# FOREVER US . . . .

# FOREVER US....

Photographs and Text by
## Walter Rinder

Celestial Arts
Millbrae, California

Celestial Arts
231 Adrian Rd.
Millbrae, CA 94030

First Printing, September 1981

Manufactured in the United States of America

**Library of Congress Cataloging in Publication Data**

Rinder, Walter
    Forever us—.

    I. Title.
PS3568.I5F64              811'.54          81-12249
ISBN 0-89087-330-5 (pbk.)                 AACR2


1   2   3   4   5   6   7      86   85   84   83   83   81

# INTRODUCTION

I believe there is a basic need for a special kind of companion in every person's lifetime. Call this companion your best friend, your lover, spouse, partner, husband or wife—your desire for this special kind of companion is a very important first step in developing your ability to love.

When you share yourself with someone else—the two of you a loving unit building a life together—the greatest fulfillment in life is possible. You can face all of life's challenges with a strong will and a courageous attitude.

When we enter this world, no one tells us that the way to love and commitment is an easy one. But building a *Forever Us* is worth all the effort and determination needed.

This book is dedicated to those of you who have found this special relationship, to those of you who are still searching, and to my lifetime companion who inspired this book.

Part I

# What Has Been Learned

# HOMEWARD BOUND

Why do we run
and keep running
away from ourselves,
away from the home
that lies within?
Many of the steps we take
lead us farther away
into an often indifferent
and demanding world,
hostile to the family of feelings
that dwell in this home.
We keep running, running
from one acceptance to another
from one person to another
from one survival to another
never stopping long enough
to honestly share a large portion
of this home within others.
We hold back our individuality
then become harnessed
to our fear of being alone.

You can stop the running away.
You can stop being frightened.
You can head back toward yourself
and maintain that tender, warm home
that lies in us all
    let us go, homeward bound.
    Let us go home!

# TRANSITION PERIOD

We enter into our tomorrows
we unwrap the unknown
by what we learn in our yesterdays.
Our present is a constant transition
between these two periods of time.
Therefore take charge of your todays . . .
be in control of this reality.

Your tomorrows can become something
to look forward to
        with excitement
                and a smile.

We must learn
    To live with ourselves
Before we can
    Lovingly
Live with others

One moment
    of your loving actions
holds more truth
Than a thousand words
    of "I love you."

# A MESSENGER CALLED LOVE

"Why are you alone and so sad," Love asked one day while He was on his journey upon Earth. He had been sent to Earth as a messenger, and He had been told to help people understand that they didn't have to feel lonely or unloved.

He said to the woman He had just met: "I am Love and I have come to touch your life in a beautiful way. I can't stay long, for I have much to do, but maybe I can help you understand why you are lonely. I have met many people whose hearts are in isolation."

The woman looked up at Love with tear-filled eyes and said, "I am tired and exhausted from my search to love and be loved. I have experienced the beginnings of loving with others but all too soon loving departed, leaving wounds that have never fully healed. The times between feeling loved are so long that I am losing the will to try again. I have come to accept my fate, and become a lonely old woman who lives on wishes and dreams."

"But you don't have to accept that fate," Love said with a gentle smile. "I have encountered many souls as lonely as yourself, and the message I bring to all of you is simply this: If you learn to love yourself, and believe that you deserve the goodness life has to offer, then you will attract loving people to you. They will want to share who you are and to help you achieve your happiness."

With these softly spoken words, Love turned to leave.

The woman, wide-eyed and excited, cried out, "Don't leave me, Love! I have so many questions I would like to ask you! So much is still a mystery to me!"

Love replied as He began to vanish down the road, "All the answers you seek are within you. Look there, for Love to replace your loneliness."

The way of love is often difficult—
few seem to complete the journey.
Don't become discouraged
as you pass people, returning.

I may be different
Because you are
        all the same.
If you were all different
Then I would be
        The same.

When your time consists of
    Appointments and schedules
There is little left
    For a new experience
        Such as I . . .

# THE JESTER

You play in the world of frivolity: making people laugh and cry, sing and dance. With your funny jests, your romantic ballads, and all the tricks of your trade, you make people contemplate the very things they would rather forget.

You are called upon to entertain, especially when people are bored or when they want their whims and fantasies acted out. At their command you are expected to perform. You are a thing of many talents upon their stage. To survive you must do what is asked, and do it promptly and well.

My jester, in your audience are those who, behind their masks of pretending, are deeply touched by your

ability to bring to the surface their emotions and their hidden desires.

When you are alone—those few precious times when no one is asking something of you—what lies within your weary, unused heart? Who do you turn to when you need a loving touch?

Maybe you are the jester in us all—crying out in silence to be free of commands, demands, obligations and expectations.

There is no applause. The curtain is shut. There are no cheers and yells. Only silence. It is your world now. You are in command. Listen!

Promises should be lived
rather than spoken . . .

# THE PATH

More leaves have fallen
than time and memory will release
during Autumn's entrance into my life.
I'd walk my dreams
and sing my wishes
imagining you beside me.
I have left many footsteps
upon the path of hope
as my life's adventures
led me to you.
I have learned not to lose faith
nor detour from that hopeful path.

Sometimes
　　fairy tales and fantasies
Hold more truth than
　　wise men's tales and reality . . .

I adore the young
           because they are the only
playmates
           for the child in me.
Age seems to banish
           youthful traits.

Only hope can bandage
a wounded heart.

Many times do I forget names
but I hold a face
within my heart, forever.

Long goodbyes
   are too painful,
short goodbyes
   leave much unsaid.
I prefer to silently, slip away
   unnoticed
until we meet again . . .


If people are to judge me
which they do . . .
let them judge me
for my intentions
my motives
my attitudes
rather than by my actions
which are too often
            misunderstood.


It is your silent misunderstanding
   I fear the most.
How should I respond to hidden feelings?
   Let your voice
      say what your heart commands.

Sometimes we present
thoughts and questions
where feelings should just
BE. . . .

To raise false hopes
        during a courtship
is both a deception
        and a cruelty.

There are times we need
to avoid situations
rather than contending with them.

We should never allow fear
to become an excuse
for not exercising
our personality
or letting ourselves
become the pawn
in another person's game.

The degree of honesty
        people show is often
measured by their independence . . .
If you perceive their independence
you can understand the depth of
        their honesty.

Few people want to make waves . . .
many would rather live
on a tideless shore
or drift upon a windless sea.
But I chose to exist
in the ever-changing activity
of thoughts and ideas,
reaching toward the endless horizon.

35

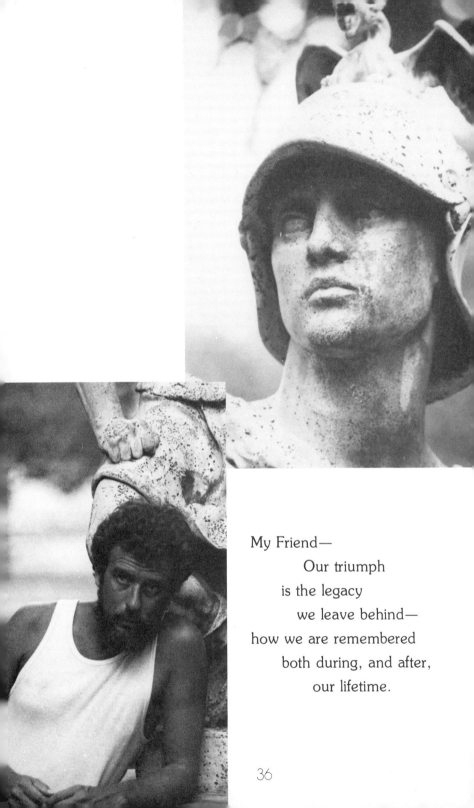

My Friend—
      Our triumph
    is the legacy
      we leave behind—
how we are remembered
      both during, and after,
        our lifetime.

Announce yourself
into your environments
into your relationships
that all eyes and ears
may recognize a being
unlike any other
   —yet—
a kindred spirit.

# Part II

# A Letter of
## Thanksgiving

The sun seldom shows itself anymore now that winter has arrived.

On this dismal, grayish, rainy morning I am sitting on the couch with a cup of coffee beside me, alone inside our mountain home by the Sandy River. Together we have enjoyed quiet moments like this so often.

I awoke a few minutes ago, feeling contemplative and a little sad to be in this beautiful house without human companionship. Isolation from city and friends can create an aloneness that is not always comfortable or desirable. But I have, of my own free will, chosen this loneliness for myself.

You are twelve hundred miles away, preparing the new home we will share. I stayed behind to fulfill the commitments I had made earlier. In less than a month, I can begin my journey to you and our new life.

I am learning now that I do not always need others around me to fulfill me or to stimulate my activities. I am learning that I can control my own time and space when it is necessary, like now. I do not need to run to the city for entertainment. I do not need television to motivate my thoughts.

I do not wish to escape from my days,
I wish to live within them.

Can't we learn to utilize better the magnificent tools we all have within us that can help us express our creativity? I am trying to use mine to continue to build a stronger personality and to develop my talents toward a more rewarding future for us.

I am writing because I want to be doing something that will strengthen me. I want to assert my energies in a positive way by practicing and becoming more proficient in my abilities. I do not want to waste time during this lonely period in my life. When I become distracted from the goals and achievements that I have planned for myself, I am not only unproductive, but I hurt myself, you, and us. I feel inner peace and satisfaction when I know that I am growing. I am motivated by the striving toward, not just the arriving at.

"Life is a mystery to unravel,
      not a problem to solve."

During a break in the rain I took a breather and chopped some wood for the fire. The physical exertion felt good.

It's important to me to share this day with you and to write you of my thoughts and experiences for you are the most special person in my life. I want us to on-going dialogue that will help us to share and enable our love to reach the highest level. I want you to know this poet who has visions, ambitions and dreams of a life of fulfillment and wonderful adventures.

May all the lives that touch ours be inspired by the love we share.

Here in Oregon I have many admirers and a few real friends. My friends are irreplacable treasures and have added immeasurable richness to my life. I do not trifle with friendship. I judge myself and others harshly during the courtship of a potential friend. To be a real friend one must be noble, honorable and giving. These are the highest virtues, and I have found them rarely. When they are absent, I feel abandoned and alone. To accept less in relationships than what you feel is good and just is to deny your own spirit.

My friends are few but vital to my existence. I hope others have found some special people who are set apart from mere acquaintances. If you believe you don't have a real friend, then look inside. The ability to have a friend, a companion, starts from within.

I've always taken pleasure in learning and experiencing, but we all have a tendency to hold tight to the image we have of ourselves. Usually when someone

(or something) tries to change this image we feel threatened. We try to resist learning something new, and possibly helpful, about ourselves. This attitude can cause rifts between us and those we care for. So we should listen thoughtfully and think honestly about what has been lovingly said to us. If we can allow our image of ourselves to be altered we can gain a greater understanding of ourselves and others. When we open ourselves up to change, and to different ideas and interests, it becomes more and more difficult to perceive ourselves as solitary the way we did when we were both single and unattached. When we chose to be together, and chose to open ourselves to change, we gave up old ways of perceiving and being.

Your presence has influenced and enhanced my love. With you, my ability to love has grown—with each passing day I love not only you, but myself, more. With you, I have been free to enjoy new experiences both physically and mentally, and every journey into the unknown has been an adventure. Some of the adventures have been good, and I cherish them. Others, less good, I have let go of but I think of them as precious lessons. I now have an image of myself as a more flexible person, one better able to accept and experience change.

My senses are constantly hungry and excited to feel more of life, to feel closer to you.

There is no end to this—only continuous beginnings that mature into eternal happiness and wonderment. We are letting go of any restrictions that prevent love from being constantly reborn out of the ashes of yesterday.

You may think me foolish for being happy with my sleepless nights, alone. Yet it is beautiful to me that I can love you so much that I feel warm and peaceful when the bed is shared by you, and feel so empty now that it is not. Only you can fill this emptiness. It is hard to learn to sleep alone again, but I would rather sleep alone than with some uncaring stranger. Your memory still clings to the sheets and pillow when I crawl into bed each night. Who can ever take your place!

I hope I can encourage people by showing them that loving is an ever-changing experience. What we do and perceive today determines our tomorrows. Our life together is a good example of this truth. If in the beginning we had been unbending, absolute or stubborn and unable to change our attitudes about loving, the chances of our building a lasting relationship would have been very slim. We committed ourselves to care enough to recognize the danger signs that could prevent the nurturing of love.

You can learn so much about yourself through me as I can through you, as long as we are not afraid to admit our weaknesses, our failings. As long as patience is our guide we can survive those times of darkness that seem beyond understanding. You once said, "Don't be in a hurry to understand everything at once. Take your time—we have a lifetime to understand." Do you remember saying those words to me? Then I didn't understand. Now I do.

There is usually a lot of confusion, clutter, and wasted energy when there is little or no order to our lives. Order is necessary to accomplish goals. We observed many times this past year that when disorder ruled our lives, we were uncertain, and mismanaged our thoughts, our actions and our reactions. As soon as order and planning took hold, we surged forward making things work for us, not against us.

This past year has been an education in survival. We allowed distractions, emotional conflicts, misunderstandings and financial pressures to detour portions of our loving. These tensions made us weak and unprepared for situations that otherwise could have been dealt with easily. Problems became exaggerated, assuming giant proportions. The energy it took to solve them took away from the order needed to change from a lifestyle of survival to one of productivity. Yes, many mistakes were made.

But we were honest and open with ourselves, with each other. We gained confidence in our ability to preserve and nurture our relationship, no matter what might happen that threatened to pull it apart.

Look at where we' are now. The exciting prospects of the coming year! We are more stable, our intentions are clearer, our goals are more defined. Intuitively, we knew this time would come, this time when all the pieces would fall into place, when we would realize the potential in each of us to contribute to this fantastic relationship. Our foundation is the solid rock of mutual caring rather than the shifting sands of self-concern.

The old ways might have been good for our yesterdays. New ways might be good for our tomorrows. The combination of both transforms our todays toward a more loving future.

The faith I have in you has no limitations, nor is it the outgrowth of an intellectual process. It is a knowing feeling from deep within my heart. We may be separated by miles, but never by a loss of faith and honor. Our love transcends conventional concepts and man-made doctrines as to how love should be lived. The only restrictions we have are those we place on ourselves by choice. The only commitments we have are

those we have made to a promise to develop our capacity to share loving actions with one another.

One of my goals is to always be where I am best able to share my love with you in ways that make you happy.

We will be together a lifetime. We are part of each other's destiny.

I am with you,
of you.
By your side,
always . . .

Written the day before Thanksgiving, 1980
Brightwood, Oregon

Part III

A
Story
About
Loving

# A STORY ABOUT LOVING

Morning yawns slowly, indiscreetly
as it meekly breaks away
from night's embrace.
Sunshine makes itself known early
and begins to stir people
toward the coming day.
I awake, refreshed and eager
to become involved
with the spontaneous experiences
that always seem to follow me.
I reach out
yearning to be exposed
to the life adventures
of each new day.

My body begins to tan
in this place of the sun
and desert sand.

The day passes
and the evening brings
a quiet sensuality
to my spirit.

Under the cover of the stars
this night
two alone souls
come together
unattached to yesterday
not committed to tomorrow.
Their spirits soar
as birds lifted
upon an invisible current
going everywhere, yet to nowhere.
Why analyze!?
        Why try to intellectualize!?
            Why try to understand!?
Let it happen as it will.

It felt wonderfully good.
Our first evening was so perfect

an attempt at sharing our heart's truth.
I remember you reached out
and touched me so affectionately that
I became a child and
let go of any adult restraints
that might prevent
the growth of something good.
In the days that followed
we grew in our awareness
that we could walk, side by side,
filling the chapters of our lives
with each other.
Years later
I am recalling many situations
that happened
which were forgotten,
as time has a way of pushing aside the past
to make way for things of the present.
How different we were
by ordinary standards:
our ages, our backgrounds, our interests!
I am an idealist,

You are a realist.
I see life through the eyes
of a romantic poet,
You see life through practical eyes.
You accept things as they are,
I think of
creating changes.
I am emotional, very active,
You are calm, relaxed.
If we had been stubborn
had not compromised,
we would not have a positive balance
of our different natures.
Then only separation
could have been predicted.
In realizing we cared
to stay together and progress
we allowed ourselves to change
our perception of ourselves.
Our love expanded
because of the direct influence of
another human being
who loves us.

Yet we did not always
understand during those moments
when understanding seemed absolutely necessary.
It was the knowledge of each other
that enabled us to become more secure
with each passing conflict
and more aware of the intentions
and reasons for our responses and actions.
We found love to be an ever-changing
ever-growing activity.
We found love to be an instrument
that someday we might master
before death passed us on
to yet another apprenticeship
of the soul.
We found honesty, and
we found trust
to be the heralds
leading us to the kingdom of love.
We discovered the traditional concept of love
so limited, so fearful of its rightness
that we began to look
inside ourselves

to look beyond convention
toward our center
for inspiration.
We found love filled our center
and we overflowed with desire
to share with each other.
We let go of those parts
of our past, of our personality
that might prevent
the constant rebirth
of the many aspects of human loving.
Because we shared together
a common foundation, a commitment,
we were not afraid to
explore the unknown, to try, to experience
changes in our attitude
where loving was concerned.
Love is an image of
what will make us happy.
Love is the present as we see
relationships forming in our lives.
Love is what we believe

now to be right and good
and beautiful in its fulfillment.
But love also dwells in the hopes
and dreams, and visions of tomorrow,
for it's in our tomorrows
that love mature
into a life-force of energy
that surpasses
anything we have come to know.
Loving is the promise
of what can be.
My love and I
stand on the threshold
of many truths
that will enable us
to live and interact with life
in a relationship conceived
through the heart's caring,
and the mind's sharing.
Love—is it enough?
The word defined, no.
The traditional meaning, no.

The expectations of love, no.
The thought of love, no.
The pattern or perception of love, no.
Our relationship is an ongoing
set of experiences
values and situations that can alter—
we bend, and pulsate, and increase,
rejuvenate, and inspire
our inner spirit to move on
and not become stagnant.
We are never satisfied with accepting
what we now know
or a mind that says
"I already know what love is."
Sitting in a Portland restaurant,
writing this,
I'm remembering the years,
our years together,
and cannot now imagine my
life without you.
We do have our own independence
our own individualism

yet what a team we make
despite our differences.

And what about us, you may ask,
is the same?
Our willingness to
care enough to
make our relationship
a lifetime experience.
I love and care for you more today than
yesterday
and will love and care for you more
tomorrow, than today. . .
as we build dreams
step by step.

# Part IV

# A
# Special
# Relationship

# THE ROMANTIC AND
# THE PRACTICAL

Both natures are inherent in us all. One or the other usually becomes predominant as we mature into adults. We live in a practical society and people today have a tendency to let go of romance and get on with the struggle of every day living by being logical and pragmatic.

The partners in a relationship can be opposites: the romantic one may take pride in creating environments and atmospheres; the practical one may pride in paying the bills on time. Both natures can flourish and a comfortable balance can be reached as the caring grows.

Romance is important, not only during sexual activity, but it helps to keep the emotional sharing meaningful, fresh and interesting.

I am very romantic by nature, and I find it disturbing at times to have to cope with predictability, routine, or the commonplace. But I have learned that disorder in life can deflect romance, so I am strengthened by a little practicality.

For me romantic interludes are essential in stimulating a relationship. A balanced blend of the romantic and the practical keeps it growing.

# DISCOVERY

We should reach deep down inside of ourselves, and not be afraid, nor resist what we find. Knowing our faults or inadequacies, our virtues or positive traits, can only propell us toward becoming better people.

We must acknowledge our own truths before we can recognize them in others.

Sharing this with each other at the beginning of a relationship can only lead to a greater capacity for loving.

# PERSPECTIVE

When we get hurt, or feel unjustly or inconsiderately treated by the one we love, it is easy to lose our perspective toward the entire relationship by focusing intensely on one moment.

Our thoughts dwell on that particular situation, magnified way beyond the significance of what happened. We lose control of our basic loving attitude, by not clarifying to ourselves the importance of the occurence within the totality of the relationship.

See the entire relationship in perspective, before you decide how you feel in acting out your re-action. Negative situations will pass. Their duration depends entirely on us.

# RESPONSIBILITY

Often we can't see the implications in refusing to be responsible for our actions. We put the blame on everything outside us, seldom on ourselves. We blame society, parents, drugs, alcohol, or the other half of our relationship. These scapegoats seem to justify our actions so we continue on our path.

As the years pass, we rationalize our negative actions from habits we have practiced for so long. After several failures in the past, we enter into a new relationship and wonder why, once again, it is not working for us. We think we're loving, and giving, and all those good things we have dreamed of.

When conflict arises, who do we blame? Who do we make feel guilty? Who ends up on trial for our actions? We're not at fault. We're always ready to justify our actions, even if they cause hurt or pain.

# THE QUESTION

What is my reason for choosing a certain person for a lifetime companion? What can I achieve with that person that I cannot with another? What is my fulfillment in being together and giving myself in commitment and devotion? What is my reason for sharing my life with a particular human being?

I love this one person!!! What does that mean? It means different things to different people. If love is our reason when we commit ourselves to a permanent relationship, then why are there so many separations? Evidently, love is not enough. Then, what is enough to bond both of us to a lasting life together?

Maybe never giving up the trying—the struggle to make it work—is the answer. Maybe it is simply a strong determination combined with flexibility and caring.

# OPPORTUNITY

We have the opportunity, at any stage of our lives to take charge of the situations and experiences that seem to block our way. We can change a negative involvement into a positive one. We can avoid situations rather than contending with them.

Freedom is knowing we always have a choice and that change is our very dear friend.

Opportunities are everywhere—change and grow!

# REBELLING

We often rebel against constructive criticism, and against new ways of looking at things.

Why are we afraid of advice or loving criticism?

Why do we often seek others who are accommodating rather than challenging?

# VIEW

Both people in a relationship should have a similar perspective on life. Their paths, though, may be somewhat different. Individual natures will take detours. They may at times walk the same path, or find another more suitable to their talents and abilities for a time, yet their basic direction is parallel.

# BLAME

In my relationships conflicts are caused by two individual concepts. One is an action and the other is a reaction, or there is a cause with an emotional effect. We sometimes disregard the effect our actions have on others. If someone responds in a hurt way, or becomes resentful, we blame him or her for the conflict that arises from the situation. Pressure and tension are the best feeding grounds for blame's accusation. And blame is always the enemy of love.

# SUCCESS

One cannot live under the glory or domination of another person's accomplishments. There has to be a mutual support, each attaining his or her degree of success. It does not have to be equal in its importance in the eyes of society or our circle of friends. But it does need to fulfill the individual natures within a unity of happiness.

Both people must feel they are successful in their sharing and fulfilling the needs of the relationship.

# CONSIDERATION

This ingredient should be an ongoing, everyday occurrence in a good relationship. It is a positive enriching habit we develop with practice and perseverance.

If we grow up with loving, thoughtful people, people with sound value systems, we learn what consideration is by the example of others.

# COMPATIBILITY

Whenever we have tried to instigate an immediate change in the other, our efforts have usually been met with resistance and resentment. When we have patiently and lovingly let the other know that we are made uncomfortable by a particulr habit, action, or attitude, and then have let go, not expecting a change overnight, our caring for the other's feelings brings forth in time the change that is needed. In a loving relationship both people are concerned about the positive effect they have on one another.

The more secure we are with ourselves, the easier it is to make the changes that make us more compatible in our relationship.

# HONESTY

This is the most important ingredient in a relationship. The more secure, and honest, I am with myself, the more able I am to express my self. I respect myself enough to want. . . .

Even though I might hurt us by being honest, I will still say what I feel. If necessary, I will explain my actions or reasons. We should be able to grow through open and honest expression. By knowing one another honestly, we will gain a greater security and confidence in our relationship.

# GIVING UP

We can feel alone or lonely because we have love-energy to share and no one to share it with. Even when we have a friend or loved one, this can happen. Sometimes we wish to assert our personal feelings, or a particular space we're in, but the other person is not in that same place with his or her fellings.

There were times in our relationship when I wanted to give up. There were times I felt you didn't appreciate my giving, nor did I feel your love or understanding. I was tired of the struggle, our conflicts mounted to such a point that I wanted to run away from them. I loved so much that they hurt with great intensity.

But each time I felt like this, I'd remember the loving times, and soon I would feel more positive and secure, reflecting on the total value of our relationship. Those few times of wanting to give up always gave way to new understandings and a greater determination to bridge our differences. I'm sure, over the years, the 'giving up' feeling will occur again, but I will know it's only temporary.

# Part V

# An
# Ever-Changing
# Perspective

Our perception—how we look at life experiences and relationships—can determine our ability to love. We all need to look at ourselves, with our eyes wide open, in the mirror of truth. Sometimes we will find that the image we are so seemingly commited to is stale and false. When we review this image, see it plain, we can get a glimpse of how it is that others see us.

A mind might contemplate itself for years and not achieve as much self-awareness as loving can teach in a day, in a moment.

My appetite for loving
is so enormous
that every day
it needs to be fed.

I am not moderate where
pleasure is concerned
nor do I ever rest
from practicing
the art of love.

If you have nothing to lose
you can always win.

Any order, complacency and security
in our lives
can break down at any time
as life continues to change,
that is why we must maintain
a friendship with ourselves.

# THAT YOU MAY KNOW THE POET FROM AFAR. . . .

How vivid is my memory of what I am about to share with you, even though it happened years ago! Some experiences we never forget. They become a permanent part of who we are.

I was on one of my cross-country trips and early one morning I drove into a small city somewhere in the deep south. I had been on the road for many weeks, I was tired and discouraged. I had been seeking inspiration for a new book and it had been difficult to find. I had met many people but had found them closed, self-concerned, uninvolved; I had hoped for more sharing and tenderness. But this was a new day, a new place, and once again I clung to the faith that someone would respond to the love I had to give.

Then, dear memory!, we met. Remember how quickly we trusted each other?

You took my hand in yours and led me through your city, showing me your special places, sharing with me your secret places. Our day, filled with so much laughter, fun and adventure, passed all too fast. The sun set, we slowed our pace. We sought out a little restaurant. We had dinner and talked about our lives before this day—this day that seemed to be a signpost to our shared destiny.

It was late that night before we found a small room in which to be together, away from peering eyes and judgmental accusations. It was poorly furnished, lit by a naked bulb dangling from the ceiling and the garish on-again, off-again, green-red-yellow flashing of neon signs advertising all sorts of escapes from society's idea of "goodness." From the tavern below came the raucous sounds of a juke box and of drunken, mindless laughter.

But this mean, abused room was transformed by our love.

The hours raced by. We fought sleep. We wanted to cherish so much more, and wanted to have so much more to cherish, when this day would be one of our yesterdays.

You were so sweet, so gentle, so innocent. You surrendered yourself to loving for the first time, giving all of yourself spontaneously—without question, without restraint.

Even now as I write this, I see your radiance lighting every corner of that dingey room. I am still drunk with that dreamer's wine of memory . . . your pleasant smile of contentment that reflected the hope that welled in your once-empty heart.

That is what loving is all about. . . .

My friend, is our life simply a collection of moments—nothing more, nothing less? Is our memory merely a storehouse for those precious moments where we go from time to time to pick among them?

Where is our true world? Is it made of only fantasies, dreams and wishes? Is it of our flesh and spirit? Do we know this world? Have we ever known it?

I celebrated my thirty-fifth birthday with the publication of my first book. At the time, I thought I was late in coming forth with my poet's voice. But now I think all those years before were years of preparation, of testing, of learning. During my youth, the designs of my poetry were beginning to form, the images of my photography were being laid out. I was restless, curious. And I was growing, however slowly, and freeing myself from society's proscriptions in order to explore my own true nature.

Through poetry and photography I have experienced truth and fallacy by directly confronting reality. But it is through love that I have come to know them.

Time is more precious to me now than it was when I was younger. I don't want to waste a moment of it. When you love, you do not waste time. My fullest moments were those when I was loving someone.

Thank you for sharing, so long ago, that fantasy of love that will always be a part of me. The rightness and goodness of loving is an everlasting adventure.

What fools we mortals be
to think we must tame
what is wild and free . . .

The only restrictions I have
are those I place on myself.

Why is it that we have to
break barriers first
before we can freely love
rather than love first
then break down barriers
because of that love.

Those times we waste
     In life
Are those times
When we turn away
     from ourselves.

# ITS OKAY TO . . .

get upset
become frustrated
feel hurt
be disappointed
break a promise or two
be forgetful
feel insecure
   uncertain
   confused
   alone
   resentful
   withdrawn . . .
But never is it okay to be indifferent
or uncaring.

We do not need a special environment
to share loving.
When we're together
our environment is created.

# GIVE LOVE A CHANCE

As you journey from yesterday into today, remember that you cannot know, predict, or see around the corner to tomorrow.

If you travel with love, layovers and detours will not detract from your journey—they will but add to the fulfillment you will experience when you reach your destination.

Give yourself a chance to love, away from the framework of habit, pattern, conformity and routine. Try not to plan ahead for every moment of your journey through life. Around the corner may be a wonderful surprise! . . . a new chance for love.

I would rather you be hurt by me
as I reveal to you my honest feeling
than have your spirit crushed
by an uncaring someone or by
a doubtful, insecure tomorrow.

Today can turn stale
if we hold on to yesterday
or cling to tomorrow.
    Let each day renew itself
with a fresh breath of life.
Two people in a relationship
should be independent,
otherwise needs and expectations,
habits and anticipations,
become a heavy mass
which will sink the building
in the quicksand of goodbye.

# ALL SHOULD KNOW

There have been times in this relationship that I have wanted to give up, to end it and be free from the turmoil, the pressures, the conflicts that result when any two people are living out their differences together.

There were times when I felt used, abused, unloved, taken advantage of and greatly misunderstood. These are the storms that test our loving, our strength of purpose, and make us stronger or weaker in our caring. They also make us more aware of the need to expand our ability to love.

Wonderful flashes of insight can arise from any disagreement or disharmony. Sometimes I've felt so foolish when a conflict occured and days later I realized my ignorance in having allowed it by not acting my loving.

My relationship has become more stable as I permit all feelings to surface and do not let guilt or stubbornness drown me in the waters of separation.

A mind can reason and question and give
answers for years upon years
but the intimacy of loving
can graduate feelings
   in a single moment
      of knowing.
When you retreat
   from self discovery
or the nature of loving
      what is left?

# FOREVER US

is not a mere reccuring image
nor an idyllic dream
but one of the most beautiful aspects
of a person's development,
springing from the embryo of loving.
All burdens
that would prevent this truth
must be laid aside from happening.

Life long companionships
that endure time and change
are *Forever Us*.

I have but one last request
my love
that you spend the rest of your life
with me

# THE CREATOR OF THIS BOOK

Standing by the front door of his Oregon home, Walter Rinder smiles at the world and wishes everyone to feel love within themselves then share that love with others.

He believes loving to be the energy force of all life, constantly creating and re-creating, building and tearing down but always in balance.

All twelve of his books, are like diaries of his life. They are written intimately and honestly. His romantic nature welcomes you into his world and simply says: This is me.

Other books by Walter Rinder. . .

AURA OF LOVE

FOLLOW YOUR HEART

FRIENDS AND LOVERS

THE HUMANNESS OF YOU

LOVE IS AN ATTITUDE

A PROMISE OF CHANGE

LOVE IS MY REASON

SPECTRUM OF LOVE

THIS TIME CALLED LIFE

WILL YOU SHARE WITH ME?

WHERE WILL I BE TOMORROW?